Women on Purpose: Bible & Business

A Study of the Book of Amos

Written & Compiled by Tonya Franklin
January 2016©

Thank You

To God, the Father for His wisdom; Jesus, my Savior for loving someone so unlovable; and to the Holy Spirit for teaching me, counseling me, and most times outright pushing me to actually do what I only dream about.

To my church family at Turning Point Mission Center for your support and prayers; love you guys to pieces! To members of the Berean SDA Church for welcoming me to exercise and be "unknown guinea pigs" of a ministry dear to my heart – which is to edify the fellowship! Your acceptance, wisdom, love, and most importantly appreciation for what I do humbles and motivates me consistently and is greatly valued.

To my children who sacrifice so much so that I can sacrifice for them. I love you, and you all are the wind beneath my wings.

To my sister-friends for your undying support of every crazy idea that I have. You come even if no one else does. Your love for me will forever be cherished.

To every woman who attended the conference bible study that sparked this book idea, thank you for allowing the Spirit to minister to you through me. You encourage me beyond what you can imagine.

About This Book:

This book actually started out as a bible study. God had imparted to me that I needed to connect my faith with my business a while back, and gave me the idea to do a bible study on prophetic messages, and how they apply to women in their professional pursuits. I admit I thought it was a far-fetched idea.

I played around with the idea, but never took out the time to really study and see how this was going to work. I put the idea on the back burner for almost a year, getting caught up with trying to run my business. God pressed the issue again and the pressing was so great, I couldn't ignore it anymore.

I chose Amos, because – well, I don't know why. But for God's reasons, this book was selected. I started a teleconference study where women would call in and we would go chapter by chapter weekly discussing this book, and pulling out nuggets of wisdom from the Lord on how this applied to us in areas of career, entrepreneurship, marriage as well as other areas of our lives.

The idea for the book came when I decided on the "fly" to offer a give-away on the last night of our bible study – so I had to do it.

I pray that you get what you need out of this book. It is intended to encourage you, strengthen you, and motivate you to do what God has been telling you to do, but you've been afraid to do it.

TABLE OF CONTENTS

Chapter 1 ~ Watch Thy Neighbor
#Covenants&Purpose

In Amos, chapter 1. This book begins with a little history about the prophet. It is interesting that Amos is not a part of the religious lineage of Levi, but God still chooses to use him anyway in such a position.

He was chosen, not because of these "normal" requirements, but because of his faithfulness to the things God had given him. He was a mere shepherd that "showed" the qualities that God felt were most necessary for a task such as this.

God's faithfulness is not contingent on legacy or birthright. Yes, He does honor that, but it is not determined by that. God is faithful to those who have a heart to be obedient to His will, and that was Amos.

The chapter gives a little background of what is happening, and we see that Amos jumps right in. First, judgment is pronounced on Israel's neighbors or adversaries. God begins the judgements as in verse 3: "For three sins…" This means, that consistently they have sinned against Him and Israel. He was expressing that He had been merciful, yet Israel's neighbors had been unwavering in oppressing them.

Damascus

Damascus was not considered a real threat to Israel. They had been defeated foes of Israel, yet, they continued to anger God through their pursuit of Israel with their advanced technology in trampling the precious city of Gilead.

> **Thought Question:** God equips us with great talents and gifts, but how do we use those gifts? How do we use them in regards to our relationships? Have you ever been in a situation when someone used their authority or position to oppress you? How did you handle it?

Gaza

This was one of Philistia's main cities. Philistia was an old-time arch-enemy of Israel since the time of the judges, and continued to be up to this time. God issues some pretty harsh judgment because Gaza had been responsible for captivating and selling them as "property" to Israel's sister, Edom.

There are two issues that God is addressing here. Number one, Gaza enslaved Israel. The type of enslavement God refers to is through idolatry and deceptive relationships. And number two, they strategically developed an alliance with Israel's family to gain power and have victory over Israel…. Which was not a good idea.

Thought Question: Have you ever dropped down your guard because you didn't think your enemy was a real threat to you, and ended up trapped in a deceptive situation that had you bound? Has this ever happened at work? Or in ministry? How did it affect your work performance? Your mentality?

Thought Question: Have you ever been betrayed by – or did you betray – your family or a professional alliance all for the sake of gaining success?

Tyre (Tyrus)

This city obtained its wealth from numerous planned associations. Tyre was once a city that was in alliance with Israel (King David), but they were heavily into idol worship. Their wealth, power and protection became a magnet to those who desired to have it, but it came at a heavy price.

As a neighbor, God chastised Tyre for betrayal of their alliance. Their desire to remain popular prompted them to shift their loyalty. They manipulated their relationship with Israel to sell whole communities of captives to Israel's family (Judah and Edom). God pronounced hat He would destroy their protective city walls by His horrible wrath (fire) that would consume Tyre's fortresses. No longer would Tyre swell in pride for their strong city walls, because God was about to expose them and their betrayal.

Edom

Biblical history tells us that Edom was a nation of people that descended from Esau and Israel descended from Jacob. Esau and Jacob were twin brothers who even from the womb, were enemies. Jacob, through the encouragement of their mother, deceived his brother Esau out of his birthright in a moment of weakness. And although Jacob had done some bad things to his brother, God still did not dismiss order and position. Israel was the chosen nation to restore man back to God. They were the ones chosen to set the example and pave the way. Esau had forgotten the covenant of his relationship with Israel. God had established the relationships of the twin brothers, but Esau had forfeited it. His relationship with Israel (Jacob) was to be prosperous for both nations. But pride, unforgiveness, jealousy, and anger overruled his judgment.

> **Thought Question:** Have you ever had a professional relationship with someone that betrayed you? How were you able to restore or repair that relationship to continue working to meet company or professional goals?

Covenants

It is never a mistake the family we are born into, the jobs we have, the bosses or co-workers that we have. God has a plan for each and every situation we encounter. It was not "by chance" or mistake that Jacob and Esau were not only brothers, but twin brothers.

God views our relationships as covenants. When we sign the dotted line to take on a project, job, marriage, etc., we have just entered a covenant. A relationship that ties us for specific purposes (I'll talk more later on this).

Jacob and Edom were to be the forerunners of Christ. They both were promised heirs of prosperity – in different ways. They were to set the example for pagan nations, but their personal rifts caused stumbling blocks in their prosperity. *We are to be careful in disregarding our covenants and relationships that God establishes to increase our territories.*

The Word says in *Amos 1:11-12* that Edom rejoiced at the oppression of Israel. This put a stench in God's nostrils, because of the covenant relationship that Edom and Israel had. Regardless of their bickering and past tensions, they were still brothers. And in God's eyes, that relationship was honorable until death.

Ammon

God's judgment on this nation was for a cruel and grotesque offense against Israel. *Amos 1:13b* says: **Because he ripped open the pregnant women of Gilead in order to extend his borders**… Wow! That's a powerful offense. The Ammonites were relentless. They did not fear their "relationship" or connection to God or anything! They were so focused and driven on their own selfish pursuits, that they ignored the covering of God's chosen people, and treated them as if they of no respect.

Purpose

What I received from these verses was about the pregnancy. This is a two-fold (possibly three-fold) message. The pregnancy was not only about natural women carrying babies, but also about spiritual women carrying spiritual babies – purpose. As a mother, our jobs are to nurture the baby in the womb by eating right, exercising, praying over our womb, and so forth. That sounds like how God wants us to cover our purpose!

You've probably heard that people say that God plants a seed in us. And I believe that He does. He plants ideas, passions, goals, etc. in us to be nurtured by His Word, prayer, good works, etc. that when it is time for it to come forth, it glorifies Him and prospers us and those that come in contact with us.

But Ammon was one who was sent to destroy that seed in Israel. How many of us encounter that same battle? How many times have we encountered a person on our job that is ALWAYS trying to undermine our growth in the company? How many of us are praying and fasting to be elevated in ministry only to have people "praying against" us or setting traps for us to fall?

Don't allow "Ammon" to rip out your purpose. God planted a purpose for you in your relationships and on your job. Protect what God has in store for you through wisdom in God's Word, prayer, fasting, and gaining strength in your covenant relationships.

Chapter 1 Empowerment

Amos was considered a common man who had no special gifts or royal heritage, but he was chosen by God to proclaim an important message.

Don't knock who God made you to be. Know that you have a purpose, and that your assignment whether it be in ministry, entrepreneurship, career, or family is important. It's not contingent on what you have, but it's based on WHO you have with you.

Seek Him in your purpose. Align yourself according to His will and purpose for you in all areas of your life. Seek God to reveal how you are to treat your relationships as covenants.

God could've used Amos in many capacities, but He used him as a prophet. Prophets were men and women who had such power behind the words they spoke because they came from God.

And that same power is in you, dear sisters! Speak prophetically over your finances, your job, your business, your family or your ministry. Declare those prophetic promises and declare protection from the trials and fiery darts that come your way from the enemy to make you forget your purpose.

When others oppress you with their skills and authority, have an Amos prophetic spirit to cover and empower you and get them in line with God. The power lies within you!

Chapter 2 ~ Standing in the Spotlight
#Profit&Position

Chapter 2 continues the judgment from God. Moab is next in the spotlight, and to give a little history on them, they are descendants from an incestuous tribe. They are of the seed of Lot and his oldest daughter (Genesis 19:30-38). Moab was known for its pagan and idol worship and for its strange sexual practices.

Although many believe that God despised Edom, because Israel was the "chosen" people, that is far from the truth. We see evidence of that here, as God renders judgment on Moab on behalf of Edom. Edom was the underdog that had a soft place in God's heart, regardless of the circumstances of their existence and character. In verse 1, God says: "**For three sins of Moab, even for four, I will not turn back my wrath because he burned, as if to lime, the bones of Edom's king...**" God still respected the covenant relationship He made with Edom (Genesis 27:39). He hated the ways of Edom, but He remained faithful to His relationship with Edom.

Judah

This is where the story gets interesting and juicy. If you've followed the story of Judah up to this point in your own personal study, you know that Judah is also a part of Israel. They separated themselves from the "family" because of leadership differences. Each "side" lauded themselves as the better of the two, causing God some serious heartburn.

Now, Judah had a problem: they failed miserably at being the right example before others. God rebukes them in judgment because they turned their back on righteousness. They were so caught up in their "chosen" status, that they neglected the very thing that put them in that position in the first place. They became prideful believing because they *had* the Law of God, that made them exempt from actually *living* the Law.

God's Law (Ten Commandments) is to show us how to treat and love God and how to treat and love our neighbor. The Law is selfless and is about service. The whole purpose of them being "chosen" was to show God's love and righteousness before pagans, so that they would be drawn back to God, but instead of drawing pagans to God, Judah was drawn by pagans away from God. They used the Law to sugar-coat and mask their detestable acts. They took advantage of their position in the Law, which we see later causes them to forfeit it all.

Judah abused their position. They sought popularity among the heathen nations to fit in (Amos 2:4) and devalued the opportunities God had given them to draw others to Him.

> **Thought Question:** Have you ever been in a position where you (or someone you know) were selected because of your education or skill, but when you had the opportunity to be a positive example, you elevated yourself and became snobbish?

> **Thought Question:** What opportunities has God given you to share His love and righteousness, but you forfeited them to be popular with your peers?

Thought Question: How much value do you place on opportunities God gives you to encourage someone on your job or in ministry, or to use your talents to help someone else succeed? Do you give your best with what you're given?

Israel: In the Spotlight

Israel was now being put on notice. God had some pretty extensive charges against them.

Even in their own past experiences of slavery, they turned around and committed the same offense! They mistreated the poor, dealt unjustly in legal matters. They followed the same suit of being influenced by pagan behaviors and sexual lasciviousness – father and son sharing the same woman (2:7)! They were no longer reverent to holy things, and while serving in temple services, took illegal collateral for bribes, and idol worship.

They sought their profit among the heathens, and disregarded the profit from the Lord. No longer were they focused on their position as a means to help someone else profit, but they were selfishly seeking their own profit.

Israel had become disrespectful of their position by abusing others they were given charge of, and the character of God – who appointed them with the authority and privilege.

Israel had the opportunity to profit from God's gift of righteousness. From time to time, God reminded them that it was He that brought them out of slavery in Egypt, but they had grown accustomed to being pampered by the favor of God. They took His grace and mercy for granted, and abused the very ones who they were supposed to care for.

Chapter 2 Empowerment

Let this mind be in you which is in Christ Jesus
(Philippians 2:5). Christ has the greatest position ever, yet
He was humble and focused on His mission to bring others
in position of authority.

His profit was the reclaiming of souls back to the Father.
Every circumstance that God allows us to be in is for the
profit of others and His glory. We are to not treat our
positions as insignificant or even boast in them for our self-
enhancement. We are to renounce the "crab in the barrel"
mentality! When God gives you a position to where you
can help someone be better and to grow, be the one who
pushes them to greater.

Beware of being like Judah. Don't allow popularity to pull
you away from where God positioned you. Stand out from
the crowd; even if that means your family, friends, co-
workers, business colleagues, etc. Your profit will be
blessed and favorable before God, and judgment will pass
from you.

Chapter 3 ~ Exposed
#PositionVersusPosture

In this chapter, Israel is being put on trial. Witnesses have come to speak up on the charges God has filed against them. Once again, in verse 1, God reminded them of His mercy by way of His response to their plea to escape from slavery in Egypt.

> **Thought Question:** How many times does God have to remind you of the sticky situations that He has gotten you out of; then you return to your vices of bondage or even worse – imprisonment of sin or disobedience?

But regardless, God pours out His love on Israel, saying that they were the only one He chose out of all of the nations upon the earth. In these verses, God gives a vivid picture of His feelings. He becomes very transparent of His love for Israel in the midst of His grief for their disobedience. He explains to them why He must deal with them just as passionately in judgment.

Verse 3 says: How can two walk together unless they agree? God is saying here that if we can't walk together, we can't be on the same purpose. Your walk mirrors your lifestyle. God is using Israel's trial as a teachable moment for them – and us. In walking with God, we are not exempt from trials or problems, but we are in a position that keeps us covered. God's plan agrees with our walk (actions), and we reap the maximum benefits of His plan for our lives. There is a purpose to our walk in our business, ministry and life in general, and God's will is "played out" in whatever we do. When we fail to walk with Him, there is a disagreement or deviation on the path to our purpose.

Thought Question: Is your lifestyle, attitude or business practices proving to be a mirror of God's character? Would God agree with how you handle your family, business, or ministry?

God explains that everything has a cause and effect. The lion doesn't growl in triumph when He hasn't caught anything. When a trumpet is blown, people react – they tremble. God says this to let Israel know, that there are consequences to their actions. Although He is merciful and He loves them beyond measure, their sins cannot go unpunished without a repentant heart.

The Prophet

Amos says here that God doesn't do anything "off-handed." He always sends a warning through His prophets. This had to be a piercing piece of news to Israel. They were known for persecuting and mocking God's messengers, and causing others to do the same.

The prophet of God was not someone who had a popular following or "job" like prophets do today. People back in those times shied away from prophets because most of the time they brought bad news. They were men and women who revealed the heart of God to the people, which most oftentimes revealed His disappointment in how they were living and treating others.

Prophets were not just death criers, they offered hope and restitution as well, but their whole sole purpose was to get the people of God to look in the mirror of the Law to get back in line with God. Godly positions aren't always glorified.

They come with great responsibility and usually require more out of you than you think you can give. Having a particular frame of mind and spiritual posture (we will talk about this next) is key to sustain the position in which you are elevated to.

Posture

Posture is defined as a position of a person's body of standing or sitting, or **a particular way of dealing with considering something or an approach or attitude**. I found it interesting another definition stated posture to mean **to behave in a way intended to impress or mislead others**.

What is your posture in the Lord? Examine your thoughts toward God and toward the assignments He gives you every day. How do you treat those assignments? Are you always hostile, snappy, secretive, malicious, stirring up discord, or hoarding information?

When we become elevated to another "physical" level in our business or ministry, we have to remember that our "spiritual" and "mental" posture must go in the opposite direction! God resists the proud. We are to have a spirit of humility. He elevates those that are humble. But oftentimes, we fail at this. We become the entrepreneur making $50,000 and our attitudes exceed also. If we are walking with God, then we are humble – regardless of the position we are in.

This was the posture of Israel. They were so comfortable in their sin because they were comfortable in their position as being chosen. Although they were chosen, they were still held responsible for their posture in God. In other words, they felt because they were God's "chosen" people that meant they were exempt from being humble and submissive to the WHOLE plan of God.

Amos called in several witnesses to testify against and watch the judgment of Israel. How humiliating!

But imagine, this is how God must have felt when the ones who were supposed to uphold God's standards of holiness and righteousness were the ones mocking and humiliating Him before others. God decided to give Israel a taste of their own medicine.

> **Thought Question:** What witnesses can God call up to testify of your character or integrity? Are there any people on your job, in ministry with you, or even in your family that can vouch for your Godly character?

God calls up the witnesses Ashdod, Egypt, and Samaria to not only testify against Israel's dealings with their *own* people, but to watch how the judgment would be carried out for their disobedience and pride (v. 9-10). God will expose us to others to be an example of how not to stray away from the path, and to give us a wakeup call.

Be mindful my dear sisters, God deals with those that have a false security because of their "position" in Him. Pride can snatch up your thinking quickly! Beware of pride because of where you think you are.

Now let's take a look at this: God was preparing to help change Israel's posture. Where once they were standing tall and mocking others, they were soon to be on their knees at the mercy of their oppressors.

The Plan

In verse 10, Amos says that the Lord declared that Israel hoarded plunder and looted the fortresses of their own. God had given them worldly riches and even more by imparting them His heart and plans.

God had provided Israel with a blueprint for bringing the heathen nations to Him. But their love for themselves, and covetousness of what seemed to be better, they strayed away from the plan.

With each position, God gives us a plan. His plans are pure and perfect. Even if we don't understand His plan for us, believe that they are perfect, and on time. Don't forfeit your position by not following the plan.

Analyzing this chapter, we see that Israel was about to lose it all. Everything they had prayed for, suffered for, and sacrificed for was about to go down in one fell swoop – because they failed to follow God's plan.

> **Thought Question:** When God elevates you in a position, do you follow His plan? Are you robbing your purpose by not following the plan?

> **Thought Question:** In your search for elevation, have you consulted God first in how to achieve it? Have you sought God on how you are to be elevated? And for what purpose?

God calls up the witnesses Ashdod, Egypt, and Samaria to not only testify against Israel's dealings with their *own* people, but to watch how the judgment would be carried out for their disobedience and pride (v. 9-10). God will expose us to others to be an example of how not to stray away from the path, and to give us a wakeup call.

Chapter 3 Empowerment

I want to encourage you that when God puts you in a position there is a purpose and a plan. The purpose is why you're there, and the plan is what you're supposed to do with the position. But to be successful and "fruitful" in that position you must have the posture of obedience and humility.

Israel had been given a wonderful position – to be the heart of God. They were chosen to be ambassadors of God's love, righteousness, and holiness. But they forfeited that position by yielding to greed, peer pressure, covetousness, pride and selfishness.

Let this not be your portion, my beloved sister. Whether you are working a 9-to-5, starting a business, revamping a business, moving into a ministry, or starting a family, remember that there is a purpose and a plan that requires a particular posture.

Chapter 4 ~ The Valley Experience
#SymbolsOfRepentance

In this chapter, Israel is being put on trial. Witnesses have come to speak up on the charges God has filed against them. Once again, in verse 1, God reminded them of His mercy by way of His response to their plea to escape from slavery in Egypt.

Why does God begin with speaking of His mercy? God, like any loving parent, gives His love first. Although He is disappointed, He gives.

Cows and Fishhooks

This is where God begins to use symbolism. In verse 1, He refers to Bashan as cows. Cows were symbolic of prosperity. He pointed out how they used their prosperity and position to oppress and crush the needy. God declared on them that they selfishly pushed their husbands to oppress others so that they could be even more prosperous!

> **Thought Question:** Have you ever used your "position" to selfishly impose on others so that you could remain comfortable in your position?

> **Thought Question:** Have you ever thought that your blessings grant you certain privileges and exemptions no matter how you conducted your lifestyle? In what ways have you sought the Lord in how to use your blessings or prosperity?

Israel had been comfortable in their own idea of self-sufficiency. They thought that their privileged position was what "kept" them, and blessed them. But God was letting them know that they were missing the entire point of being blessed by Him. It wasn't for their own sufficiency – but to follow the plan, which was to draw others to Him.

The second symbol we see in this chapter is the fishhook. A fishhook was used to entrap a fish. Fishhooks is translated in various meanings from the Hebrew/Arabic languages. The loose translations refer to giving up to (as in putting in a pot to be boiled to be offered) being detained for a purpose, and it also translates to mean: to be captured.

So what was God saying here? God prophetically used Amos to say that Israel was going to be held up. Do you remember the old conveyor belt? Sometimes a product would get snagged and get held back from moving forward with the others. And after a while, it would finally give way, releasing the product to get back on the belt to go in the direction it was supposed to go. This is what God was trying to tell Israel. They were going to be detained. The succession of events to come would have Israel in holding or limbo for a while until they started listening to Him.

Israel had experienced various tumultuous things such as enslavement, famine, drought, desecration of land, insect plagues and more. Yet, they remained intolerant to the warning signs that God had given them through these experiences. Their repentance had become routine, thus, they still failed to heed the voice and learn their lessons. They saw these experiences as mere hiccups to their blessings and status as the "chosen people" of God.

In His frustration with their inability and callous hearts to listen, God in turn goads them on by telling them to just go ahead and sin, since they love it so much. God was saying this because He would rather they be hot or cold for Him (Revelation 3:15-16). There is no middle ground – no serving Him in deed, yet serving self and Satan in heart.

> **Thought Question:** Has someone subordinate to you tried to warn you or tell you of a mistake you made? How did your posture (Chapter 3) determine your reaction to them pointing that out to you?

He rebukes them harshly by reminding them of their ungratefulness (4:6-8), and no matter how much He blessed and provided for them, they still had not returned to Him. He even reminds them of how He allowed trials to come upon them to get their attention, and they still ignored it and did what they loved to do best – sin against Him.

> **Thought Question:** Has prosperity ever blinded you? When God allowed trials to come, did you recognize that He was getting your attention, and did you listen, or did you in your selfishness move farther away from God?

They failed to see God's love for them in their valley experiences. They saw it as an inconvenience, and missed the mark! Their valley experiences were opportunities for them to reflect on themselves, and listen to God.

> **Thought Question:** How do you see trials? Do you view them as God punishing you, holding you back, or being sadistic toward you striving to prosper?

Trials come for various reasons. In business and ministry, the valley experiences are to get our attention, they are to sit us down so we can listen to what God has planned for us.

Many times we view our valley experiences in a negative mindset; but if we sit back and listen for God (even when He doesn't say anything), He will answer, give us comfort or peace to endure – and learn in the process of the experience. Our experiences are to make us better, even if those experiences sometimes hurt.

Chapter 4 Empowerment

God always has our best interests at heart. He knows what we need, more than we know what we want. God's relationship or covenant with us is not by duty because He's God and He has to love us, but it is because of His desire to be in a relationship with us. He wants to love us! And this is why it hurts Him so much when we step out of His will. His will is His blueprint for a good marriage between Him and us.

God's plan for our lives is so complex, yet so easy. Living in the flesh seems so good to us, but it has horrible consequences. The plan God has for us is not only for us, but for others to be drawn to Him. We are ambassadors – representatives of God, and others are either drawn to Him or repelled against Him by our example.

We are reliant on God for everything, and should not take God's relationship or blessing for granted. In believing that we are self-sufficient, we turn away the affection that God gives to us daily by showering His love, mercy, and protection. Our blessings are not protection from the sting of sin, but a show of God's love for us.

God blesses us not to become independent of Him once we've got the blessing, but He desires us to lean on Him even more! We need Him as we move to our next level. The greater the level, the more that God has in store for us, and we must be even closer to Him, knowing our purpose, and following the plan.

Even when we have valley experiences, they are not always punishment because of wrongdoing, but may be the opportunity that God gets to quiet and slow us down from the cares of life, so that we may hear Him, and to get prepared for the next season in the plan He has established for our lives. And if those experiences are because we are out of God's will, we should have a spirit of repentance and humility, that we recognize our error and get back in line!

God's plan is perfect, and His love for us is beyond what we could ever, ever imagine. Just as He is passionate about loving us, He is even more passionate about us doing what is right.

Chapter 5 ~ The Call to Repentance
#SeekHimAndLive

Chapter 5 is the beginning of the climax of the entire book.
God has issued the charge, provided the witnesses, and now
the judgment comes – no, the call to change comes. This is
a weird turn of events. God has expressed His anger, but
He remembers the soft spot He has for Israel. He
remembers His first love back at their courtship (in Egypt),
and appeals to them one more time through His prophet
Amos.

Although Jeremiah is called the "Weeping Prophet," Amos
laments bitterly on behalf of God to Israel. In the first two
verses Amos cries out on the spiritual state of Israel.

Walk On Purpose

I find it interesting in verse 3 how God responds that out of
1,000 strong, only 100 will be left. Even in spiritual and
judgmental matters, God will claim a tithe!

The purpose God gives us is a gift; not a duty. He equips us
before our birth with what we need to fulfill it. Each
woman's purpose is unique, and given in careful and
special dedication. Don't abuse your purpose; God will get
back what belongs to Him. Even our purpose is gifted as a
tithe.

There are many times we complain about spending too
much time at church or in ministry, but we fail to realize
that God doesn't ask for much from us – only a small
fraction of 10 percent. We treat God's requests as
inconveniences to our busy and important lives.

We fail to understand that without God's leading, without His instruction, and without His gifting to us we have and are nothing. Our businesses will fail, our professional pursuits (i.e. college, job training, skill assessments, etc.) and our relationships will ultimately fail us. There is no security in our own doings without Him, so why would we treat God as a second-hand thought, instead of a priority? Without God to plant our purpose in us and give us instructions, we would not even have the foggiest clue on how to walk in our purpose or to do it on purpose.

Beware of Complacency

Amos begs Israel to seek God and live, not to trust in religion that soothes carnal desires (Amos 5:4-5). Again he begs: seek God and live, because religion cannot save them from the judgment of God (Amos 5:6). Religion is important, but having a spiritual relationship is vital. It does not shield us from the hard times of life, but it serves as support and strength in those hard times. Israel had their thinking all backwards. They believed that their religion was tied to their purpose, which made them become complacent (lazy) in nurturing their relationship with God. It just became a part of their to-do list, instead of their love and strength-building time.

> **Thought Question:** How many times does God plead for us to turn around when we've strayed from our purpose?

> **Thought Question:** How do you view your relationship with God? Do you see it as just another part of your list of things to get done, or do you look forward to seeing Him and spending time with Him?

Thought Question: How do you reflect your relationship with God to the relationships you have on your job, with others in ministry, or in your personal or professional relationships? How are they similar, or different?

God speaks with so much passion and hurt in His heart with conviction to Israel of how they turn justice into bitterness throwing righteousness to the ground. He serves as our mirror of righteousness and how to handle situations correctly, and when we choose to do things our own way, it as if we throw God's wisdom to the ground as if it is trash!

Thought Question: What is your reaction when God allows you to go through valley experiences? Do you heed the call to seek Him in decisions for your business, your ministry or on your job when you encounter difficult situations?

God tells Israel that although they build stone mansions, they would not have the opportunity to live in them (5:11). Status or privilege doesn't protect you from judgment or hard trials. Hard trials come to humble you to acknowledge and hear from God. He points out that no sin they have committed is hidden from Him (5:12).

And again, God pleads with Israel to seek God and turn away from evil! Once again He pleads with Israel to turn away from evil – to get back on the path of the plan! Repent, and move out of the comfort zone of their sin! Beware of the wealth we strive and sacrifice to build, because if we're not "on purpose" and doing the will of God; He snatches it from us.

Thought Question: How many times has God pleaded with us to change our direction and warned us and we did not listen? What was the outcome? What do you think would have happened if you had listened to God's warning?

God presents His plea in an aggravated reprimand. The people asked for God's justice in times past, but didn't realize that the justice wasn't just for their enemies, but for them as well. In other words, God was telling them that they didn't know what they were asking for.

Thought Question: How many times has God pleaded with us to change our direction and warned us and we did not listen? What was the outcome? What do you think would have happened if you had listened to God's warning?

Thought Question: In prayer on behalf of a situation, do you seek God on the role you played or do you just pray for God to "fix" the other party involved?

Although God is angry and fed up, He still is merciful. At the first sign of His anger, He could have allowed oppression to come upon them instantly – or even destruction. But be mindful that this prophecy comes to pass nearly 40 years later! Early on, God was giving them warning and "probation" to get back in His will; but would they heed the warnings from Him through Amos?

Chapter 5 Empowerment

Our relationship with God is very important to Him. Can you imagine marrying someone and thinking that the both of you are committed to being faithful to one another, sharing the same dreams and goals, and wanting some of the same things out of life; and then find out that they are just with you out of convenience? They have no interest in what you want out of life. They don't talk to you unless they want you to cook dinner, or they only show you affection when they have nothing else to do? This is how God felt that Israel treated Him.

As women, we are so busy! We have so many things we have to do and are trying to do, but God still needs His time. And He wants you to *want* that time, not just because you "have to do it."

Have you experienced silence or being uncomfortable in God's presence because you're not sure how to approach Him? Remember how it was when the first time you met your husband or significant other? Did you just quit the relationship because of the awkwardness, or did you continue to get to know Him to find out more? Yes, you probably did, and after getting to know him, you realized you both had some things in common, and the more time you spent with him, the more comfortable you got to be around him. Guess what, beloved sisters, that's how God is. He knows you, but He wants you to get to know Him. He doesn't want you to go by what you've heard others say about Him – find out on your own. Don't allow religion to be a "cover up" for really getting to know God. Religion won't save you, and it won't substitute for the real thing.

If you're in a slump in where you are in your marriage, your ministry, your business, or your career – don't worry. God has more to share with you. Spend more time with Him. He desires to help you walk in your purpose, so that you can begin to walk *on* purpose.

Chapter 6 ~ Lifestyle of the Heart
#BewareOfComplacency

In this chapter, we continue to hear God's rebuke on both Judah and Israel. God shares this rebuke on both nations collectively, although they consider themselves apart.

God's anger is directed at the condition of their hearts. Both nations have attained great wealth and respect from surrounding nations despite their enemies, and it was all due to God's favor on their lives and respect for the covenants He established with their forefathers – not their impassiveness to His will.

These nations allowed "privilege" to give them a false security with God as well as pride in their hearts in how they used their wealth.

Amos goes back to the witnesses God presented earlier (6:2) to present even more reflection. Although God have given them wealth and victories against their enemies, this was not the go-ahead to take advantage of the favor He placed on them to become prideful. Just as God blessed them, He had also blessed Calneh, Hamath, and Philistia.

We become misguided in thinking that position automatically yields favor and blessings. But that is so far from the truth. Many times we are riding on the coattail of someone else's covenant and obedience to God (Example: Israel on the promises God made to Abraham and David). But we can't become complacent in that, for the grace of that overflow soon runs out and God yearns fresh sacrifices.

Amos dishes out some serious offenses that range from striking fear into the people (lauding power over weaker people), ignoring the disrespect to their ancestors to remain comfortable in their lifestyle.

In verse 5, Amos mentions their worship. Israel lauded King David as one of the heralds of pure praise and worship unto God, and because they were "descendants," they imitated this style of worship. Amos points out that their worship wasn't sincere, but it was a ritual to show enough allegiance to God while they continued to sin against Him and worship their idol gods that made them comfortable in their sin.

God isn't against prosperity and wealth (Isaiah 58:14). But He does have a problem with misusing the opportunities He gives us to bless others or glorify Him with our prosperity.

> **Thought Question:** How many times has God pleaded with you to change your direction, warned you and you did not listen? What was the outcome? What do you think would have happened if you had listened to God's warning?

Complacency dulls our senses. We become relaxed and miss out on opportunities God may put in our paths to fulfill our purpose. This was one of Israel's problems. They were so busy enjoying the luxury of having ivory, choice lamb, and finest lotions that they became blinded to the people who needed to be encouraged and helped.

God said He hated Jacob's pride. He declared that city would be delivered up completely. They were going to be reduced to the "bare essentials" so that they would be humbled and finally listen to what God had to say.

Even in their complacency, they knew that God wasn't pleased. They just took His mercy for granted! They even said that even during times of calamity or grief, no one should mention God's name for fear of being judged also.[1]

Isn't it ironic that these two nations have called themselves forsaking their covenant relationship with each other, but their actions tend to mirror one another? Remember in Chapter 1, we talked about covenant connections, and how our destinies are connected to the people God has covenanted us in. No matter how much these two "sisters" tried to NOT be like one another, they still managed to behave in like-manner. Don't forget this! What God puts together, it is for a divine purpose to your next level.

> **Thought Question:** Have you done a good job, but your heart wasn't in it? How did you feel about the work you did? How did you feel about the person you did the work for? Do you think that if you thought differently, you would have given more than half-hearted service?

> **Thought Question:** What does your work ethic say about your relationship with God?

---

[1] *Chapter 6 Commentary, Life Application Study Bible (NIV).* Tyndale and Zondervan, 1991.

Chapter 6 Empowerment

We use the excuse all the time: "God knows my heart" as a way to live how we want to, but not give any real commitment. The sad truth is that God does know our hearts. He knows that when we work if we're sincere or if we're just performing rituals to say we've done something.

God wants us to be vessels of integrity. No matter what it is – whether it is on our jobs, in our relationships, ministry, or businesses – God wants us to do it with sincerity and with purpose. And no matter what facet it is, everything we do should be to glorify the gifts that God has given us. The spotlight shouldn't be on our rituals or works, but on the One who gave them to us.

In working with integrity and passion, we will have a renewed vigor and eagerness to grow because of our experiences. Our wealth is not what defines us, but it is our character that defines our wealth. And as the saying goes, experience is the best teacher. Allowing God to teach us through valley experiences and opportunities is what helps us to discover our purpose that reveals the plan God has for us as His daughters.

Chapter 7 ~ Symbols of Judgment
#Authority

We know prophecy deals with a lot of symbolism, and this book of the Bible doesn't disappoint us. We talked earlier about how symbolism was used to describe the condition of Israel; now, we're going to take a look at how God uses symbolism to describe how He plans to deal with Israel.

Locusts

I did a little research about locusts, and this is what stuck out to me. In low numbers, they behave as grasshoppers tending individually. But in high numbers as they mature, they perform as marching bands or swarm in the mode as if they are an entity.[2]

Isn't that how God operates when something great is about to happen? Take a look at Christ's baptism? All three of the Godhead were present (Matthew 3:13-17). There is something powerful in having God the Father, Son and Holy Spirit!

Amos obviously knew this, and he cried out on Israel's behalf stating that Israel was defenseless against this kind of power (7:1-2). God, though angry and hurt, was still in love with Israel and He relented to Amos' intercession.

---

[2] "FAO Desert Locust Guidelines- Food and Agriculture" Fao.org

Fire

The next vision Amos saw was the Lord calling down fire. We know that fire is consuming and changes the property of a thing, and also changes the appearance of it. It symbolizes God's Spirit burning sin away.

God was intending to change the appearance and property of Israel. They were about to be unrecognizable! Their position and authority were about to altered completely by God's judgment.

When we build without God, we are bound to experience the "fire." God will re-route everything – even destroying – for you to get back in line with your purpose.

> **Thought Question:** In business, you go through many changes. Have you made mistakes that God may have had to consume it from the "roots" or just change it all together?

Plumb line

The final vision was of a plumb line. A plumb line is a tool that is used mainly by carpenters or architects to insure that objects are aligned or upright. This symbol is in reference to the law of God. God promises us that our standard to be judged when He returns will be His law. The plumb line measure up against our foundation (lifestyle and works) to see if we are lined up with His righteousness and upright in His love.

> **Thought Question:** When you evaluate yourself, how do you measure up against God's righteousness? What is your foundation built upon?

Amaziah v. Amos

Amaziah, the priest comes into the picture sending a message to Jeroboam, the king of Israel. Now, Amaziah is one of God's representatives. He is the intercessor of God's people. But watch what he does. He sends a message that Amos is raising a conspiracy against the king with his prophecies from God.

I find it amazing that Amaziah, who is supposed to be a man of God and Amos is a man of God, but they are not on one accord in hearing from God. Why do you think that Amaziah didn't get the message from the prophecies? It is possible that Amaziah was dealing with personal issues with Amos' position and assignment, because it conflicted with his own agenda that had little or nothing to do with what God wanted. So in his haste to confuse Amos' assignment, he stirred up fear in Jeroboam with lies.

Being on one accord with God is important. And being on one accord with business associates and fellow yokeman in ministry is just as important. Unification does NOT always mean you agree on the methods or ideas, but you are in harmony in purpose, and if you are united to compromise selfish agendas and you desire to communicate, you prevent the spirit of conflict from arising.

> **Thought Question:** Have you ever had someone who was a colleague or teammate to stir up dissension when you were on task doing something that was not popular, but it was what you were supposed to do? How did you deal with the situation when lies were told on you for doing what was right?

Amaziah tries to get rid of Amos by banishing him from prophesying in Bethel. But, Amaziah didn't understand that Amos' assignment didn't come approved from the prophets of Israel. Amos' assignment was signed, sealed, and approved by God! When God places you on assignment, you are to move forward as He leads.

Amos informed Amaziah that he wasn't appointed because of lineage or privilege, but because God appointed him. Amos knew his authority was given to him by God, and no bullying would frighten him off from doing the work of God (7:14-15). Amaziah's authority was allowed by God, but it wasn't established. He wasn't chosen to carry out the incredible mission of sounding the alarm of repentance to Israel.

> **Thought Question:** When God appoints you to a position or mission, does your response to adversity reflect you knowing who gave you the authority to handle business? Do you stand boldly in knowing who appointed you and you continue the work or are you timid and bow down to pressure from others who speak against your work?

Amos boldly rebukes Amaziah harshly because he was placed in the position to fulfill the purpose of bringing the people closer to God. But Amaziah was caught up in the popularity of the position. Pride elevated Amaziah into "false authority." His authority had been reduced because of his pride and sin, so the assignment had been passed on to Amos.

> **Thought Question:** Do you know where your authority comes from? Have you become prideful because you've been elevated in your career, in ministry, or in your

business? Do you feel that you have authority to oppress or suppress others subordinate to you? Does God approve of oppression?

Amaziah missed it. He missed his purpose in God. His purpose wasn't to elevate his position, but to glorify God in the position.

Chapter 7 Empowerment

Authority is the act of being in charge to administer the law or the right to tell someone what to do. Daughters, you are going to encounter many people in your life that believe because they are in a "position," that grants them authority over you. But remember this, Israel's pride had become so enlarged and their sin so grievous that they had forgotten about the true Source of their authority. No longer did they have that privilege because their hearts were turned away from God.

Have a bold spirit like Amos. Know that your position does not define your authority. You may be just a shepherd with no priestly heritage or educated background, but if God spoke it to you and put you there, you are meant to be there. Your validation doesn't come from man, it comes from God. When the fires of life come upon you, remember that God is with you. Intercede even on your own behalf, and watch how God turns things around! Rely on mercy and love shown to us in situations during our immature years to build upon during harder tests and trials in latter years. God sends trials to humble us and grow us up in our faith to rely on Him and to walk in His will.

Be careful to not be as Ammon who relied on false security. Understand that your authority comes from God alone. He plants purpose in you, ordains and gives you your marching orders, and then He sends you on assignment. Your job, career, ministry, business or family is not by accident. This is the assignment God has given to you! Don't be like Amaziah and allow sinfulness, pride, disobedience, fear, doubt or immaturity to cause you to miss out on opportunities meant to bless you and build up others.

When "Amaziahs" come up against you, remain humble yet stand strong. Continue with your mission! God has a wall of protection around you.

The Word of God should always be our standard in how we operate and view our position and authority. It is not because our mother held the positon prior to us or because we are so smart that we are in the position we are in, but by the will of God that has appointed us. Remember, our authority doesn't lie in worldly gains and pursuits. It rests in God.

Chapter 8 ~ Judgment Cometh
#SummerFruit

This chapter gives more substance to the judgment that is about to be handed to Israel. They are not prepared for this message from Amos, because they don't see the manifestation coming to pass at the present moment while they are still enjoying the fruit of their sinful labor, their lack of godly worship, fulfilling their lusts and massaging their prideful hearts. But even as Amos delivers this word, the hearts of the people tremor, thinking of the possibilities of Amos' messages becoming true.

Amos sees another vision, and it is a vision of a basket of ripe fruit. This is symbolic of Israel's works (deeds) for and against God. The Father calls into view the deeds of Israel again. He compares their deeds with His standard (the commandments). The ripe fruit is usually ready to be picked and inspected to be sold or eaten. So now, Israel's deeds are ready to be picked, inspected, and received – or discarded.

God examines our "fruit" daily. Even when we are not thinking about what we do, God examines it against His Word. We have no excuse to not live holy and righteous. We have no excuse to not seek purpose and walk in the plan. He has given us all that we need, and has even exceeded it to give us more! Sisters, we are pampered by God. He pours abundantly into us when we open up to Him. See, this was Israel's problem. They felt they had enough of God and when they shut off the spout, they dried up and their fruit looked good and ready on the outside, but when God inspected their "fruit," it was rotten to the core.

> **Thought Question:** When was the last time you did a self-examination of your fruit? Have you found that you are lacking in areas of faithfulness, obedience, submission, and serving others? *Examine your own fruit – and turn around! Repent, seek Him and live!*

God tells Amos in this vision that the worship songs will come to an end. There will be no more shaking and faking! There will be no more "acting" holy. Notice in His sharp rebuke, He doesn't even call them by their name Israel, but by their deeds: "You who trample the needy and do away with the poor of the land" (8:4 NIV). *Have you ever been so angry with someone that you didn't even call them by their name, you just shouted out the things they did to hurt you?*

But it doesn't stop there. Israel took their relationship with God for granted, and in turn God rebuked them for not taking sacred time that He set aside to be with (vv. 5-6). How were they to receive instruction or wisdom if they never spent time communicating with Him? They relied on their past instructions to carry them, but when you are entering a new season, you have to receive the next level of instructions. Israel had lost that desire to spend time with God, and began to listen to their own wisdom and judgment.

> **Thought Question:** Have you ever dishonored God's time with you by rushing quiet time with God, because you are so busy trying to prosper wealth? How important do you think it is to connect with God in your career, business, ministry or relationships? What does God want to say to you, but you're just too busy to hear?

Thought Question: Have you forfeited time to receive instruction because of your self-sufficiency on what you "already" knew? What important pieces of your career or ministry purpose did you realize you missed out on by forfeited that time? How did it effect you going to the next level?

Earthquakes

God lets Israel know that their good times are about to be over. Their sweet melodies of worship are about to be exchanged for wailing of mercy. The trembles of the earth (earthquakes) will come and they will want to repent (v.8). Earthquakes produce splits in the earth. God is also referring to a "spiritual" earthquake. These type of earthquakes come when hardship and bad things happen to us. Most times, if we're honest, we pull away from God. Our sin or lack of faith tends to separate us because we're looking with our natural eyes. This is what Israel was going to face. They had done it time and time before, and God knew they would do it again. Instead of running to God, they allowed their sin and faithlessness to divide them from the One who could restore them whole.

Thought Question: How do you handle "spiritual" earthquakes? When trials come upon you, do you separate from God with a heart hardened against His warning to you, or do you run to Him with a spirit of humility and pleading to be closer to Him?

Spiritual earthquakes happen more often than not, and can be true tests of our faith. But I want to help you understand that our purpose is not "tied" into our earthquake experiences. During these times, we may feel separated from God, but it is in the breaking that God works the best in us.

Famine

In verses 9-14, Amos sounds the alarm! God tells him to let Israel know that there will be famine in the land. This is more of a spiritual famine that God is emphasizing than a literal one. God tells them in verse 11b: *"not a famine of food or a thirst of water, but a famine of hearing the words of the Lord.* (NIV)" Oh, how horrible! Israel was about to experience a silence like never before. There would be no prophet harassing them about living holy, no priests interceding on behalf for their sins, and no teachers in the synagogue giving them words of hope – nothing. They were about to be dry, parched, and brittle. They would go from place to place that seemed full of nourishment, but would only find emptiness and hunger. They would go hungry, and never be able to find food to sustain them. Israel didn't appreciate it when they had it, so God was going to take it away from them. They were about to find out what it really meant to be spiritually starving.

> **Thought Question:** Have you ever been in a season when you desperately needed answers from God and there was only silence? Did you ever wonder why the encouragement of the Word was void in your life? How were you able to function in matters of life when you didn't hear from God? Did you find other vices to help you deal or cope with your problems?

Chapter 8 Empowerment

Be encouraged my sweet sisters. If this chapter has mirrored your life lately, there is still hope! This is the warning, the sound of the alarm for you to get back in line with God. The fruit you've produced thus far is just the beginning. There are more seeds to plant – such as encouraging others, praying for and with others, making honest decisions, and caring for the needs of others without condition. Even if there is silence, God desires to still receive your repentant heart. He still desires to love on you and through you.

Don't take God's love and mercy for granted. If you're going in the wrong direction, turn around. Repent and seek Him even more. Don't allow your melodies of praise and worship to become dirges of mourning. Your summer fruit of unrighteousness can cause you to lose your joy, peace, and love. Examine yourself and be persistent with God. Have a Jacob spirit (Genesis 32:22-28)! If you are having a season of famine or a valley experience, continue to seek God with the Word that is in your heart. Don't allow the "earthquakes" of disobedience, distraction, busyness, and sin separate you from your purpose and the walk that God has given to you.

Additional Keys to Moving Forward:

To turn around is to **develop your prayer life:** talk to God daily, not out of duty or responsibility, but out of love and a desperate need for being in His presence; **develop a life of bible study:** get in God's word! It is His love letter to you. Even the harsh pieces have sprinkles of life and love. Learn more about the God who not only created you, but created your purpose and designed your walk with Him; and **develop a heart of service:** no matter if you're struggling in your career or even your education.

Learn how to serve others. God rebuked Israel harshly in Chapter 8 for mistreating the poor and cheating people out of their money (falsifying balances). Our duty is to love our neighbor as much as we love God; there is no way around it. Even the people that are hard to love, God wants us to develop a love for them through heart-felt service. You can do it!

Chapter 9 ~ Sound The Alarm
#Redemption

At the close of every prophetic message that God gives, He gives a message of hope and redemption. This is God's purpose in every prophecy! He desires not to destroy us, but that we may be saved (2 Peter 3:9) and have joy more abundantly. But He is holy, and sin cannot dwell in His presence; it must be destroyed.

The headline of this chapter is about Israel's destruction, and it is hard with the natural eye to see how God could even begin to sprinkle hope in this final chapter. But we will see that even in His justice, He still has a soft spot of mercy.

Part-Time Lovers

Amos says he sees the Lord in a dream standing by His altar giving instruction to an angel to bring destruction to the people. There are instructions of death, enslavement, humility, and exile. He reminds Amos through this dream that He is God, and even in this, He is just. He further reminds Amos of how He showed no favoritism to Israel, and that what He is about to do is only what is right and necessary for them to bring them back to purpose. Although God loved Israel with a love that cannot even be explained or penned, Israel chose to cling to their sin. Their love for their own self-righteousness was more important than their love for God. They treated God as a part-time lover, and God said it was over.

Thought Question: Have you gotten fed up with being a part-time lover with God? Is doing your own thing more important than following God's purpose and plan? Do you only seek God when it's convenient or when you feel like doing it?

Thought Question: Do you seek God to put on a show for others to believe you're more than you really are? Have you pretended to seek God, but inwardly you haven't spoken with God in a while?

Thought Question: How "hot" is your relationship with God? Does it show in your relationships with your employees, co-workers, church members, ministry associates, or family and friends?

Restore

At the beginning of the chapter we see God passing down the judgment, but God loved Israel so much, that it grieved Him to even do it. It wrenched His heart, as if a piece of it had been snatched from His very chest. But God is a God of justice, and sin must be handled.

Now look at what He says in verse 11, there is a huge shift! He says that He's going to restore them. The season of destruction and famine wouldn't last forever. He would restore what was lost to them, if they just would seek Him. Learn their lesson and move ahead!

Thought Question: Have you ever wondered if you would just repent and seek God, that He would restore to you what you've lost or even give you something even better? Have you ever had to go through a season of famine and destruction, and God's wisdom just tells you to be patient and obedient because He's going to restore you?

He says in verse 13: "The days are coming (NIV)." This was good news to Israel's ears. Even though they would have rather God not proclaim any judgment at all, at least they had some ray of hope. He ends by telling them that even though they would be uprooted, they would be replanted to never be uprooted again. He foreshadows the coming of Christ (David's tent) who will come over 300 years later to rebuild so that even the Gentiles (remnant of Edom) would bear the name of the Lord.

Chapter 9 Empowerment

Wow! God took us through this entire book, and left no stone unturned. He exposed Israel of their deceit, wickedness, nonchalant worship, indifference to others, selfishness, and haphazard relationship with Him. But in the end, He gave them hope. This book may have come to a close, but the book of your life has not. Chapters begin and end, but there is still more for you.

Don't beat yourself up over past mistakes, sins, and even current ones. God is in the business of restoring and rebooting. If you've hit a slump in your worship and relationship with Him, get back up. If you've been that hard-to-get-along-with supervisor or co-worker, repent. If you've been the wife or mother from hell, seek God for a turn-around. God provides us hope at the end of it all.

Seasons of hard times come so that we can look to the hills where our help comes from. They are periods of reflection on how good He's been, and how much He has even in store for us in the future.

He has promised to restore the house of David, and God never fails to keep His promises. Even when we are not faithful, God is still faithful. He still is a God of love and mercy, but He is also a God of holiness and justice. Allow God to clean out the areas of sin or disobedience in your life so that you may walk in your purpose on purpose.

Sister To Sister ~ A Note of Love and Encouragement

I want to first thank you for purchasing this book, and I look forward to sharing more of God's heart with you in studies to come.

I would like to leave this note with you: When God created you as a woman, He did not make a mistake. It was not a second choice decision. Eve was created to be a helper, and to fulfill divine order in the Earth. And that is what you are also. God created you with intuition (the secret language of the Holy Spirit), nurturing, compassion, passions, and tenacity. He created you to be the "emotional" side of Him. In His image we are the forgiving, loving, and life giving creation.

Trust God. As women, we are pulled in hundreds of directions doing so many things and bearing so many burdens. But know this, that whatever you put your hand to do, do it the glory of God and He will bless it!

Don't allow your faith to fail you on this journey that God has placed you on. It matters not where you come from; God has equipped you for such a time as this. You are there by design, and not by circumstance or mistake! Even the bad will turn around for your good if you faint not.

Bless others, take advantage of the opportunities God gives you to draw others to Him, remember that blood is thicker than water – cherish your family covenants, and remember that your authority comes from the Lord.

You are a powerful force to be reckoned with, and that's why the enemy wants to get inside your head and spirit to abort your purpose before it is even born!

Prophesy with authority over your royal place in the earth, and position in the spirit. Your family, business, career, or ministry will be blessed because God ordained it to be so. Forget not the valley experiences that God has allowed you to go through. It has not been for nothing, but has been permitted to strengthen you and prepare you for the next level. Remember, my beloved sisters, you are a woman on purpose to be on purpose for Him.

Prayer:

Dear God, cleanse my heart. I choose You to be Lord of my life and the defender of my purpose. I ask that You save me from the sin that seeks to keep me from being wholly Yours. You have made me fearfully and wonderfully in Your image, and with all my frailties, You still have chosen me to carry out a purpose on the earth. I ask that you remove fear, doubt, insecurity, negativity from my family and peers, and to replace with authority, royalty and boldness for You. I thank You for all You've done, and all that You will do beyond what I can even imagine. In Jesus' name, I pray Amen.

There's More…
Motivational & Empowerment Scriptures

Work hard… *Genesis 2:15*

Every position has its purpose. Your position is significant… *Exodus 35:35*

Do business with integrity. God honors fairness… *Deuteronomy 25:13-15*

Seek to know your position and prepare your posture for it… *Proverbs 22:16*

Give your all for God. Treat your subordinates and insubordinates as you would God… *Colossians 2:23*

Honor your professional relationships. Treat others like you want to be treated… *Matthew 7:12*

Whatever assignment God gives you, He has already empowered you to handle it… *Philippians 4:13*

You were born with a purpose that will shape the nations… *Exodus 9:16*

You were called to a standard higher than even your own desires, because of God's love for you… *2 Timothy 1:9*

Your skills are blessed by God… *Deuteronomy 33:11*

About the Author:

Tonya has been writing since the age of 13, and has had a love for words ever since. She serves as a contributing writer for various e-zine publications, and is currently working on two other writings for small businesses as well as a non-fiction book for publication.

The author of "Good Customer Service Tips for Entrepreneurs," she is the Chief Administrative Officer/Owner of UpWrite Solutions, LLC that offers virtual services in marketing, event consulting, and basic office administration. She is a native Mississippian, but has also lived abroad in Europe. She has a love for food, teaching, and reading.

Website: www.tonyadfranklin.com
Facebook: www.facebook.com/tonyathewriter
Instagram: www.instagram.com/upwritesolutions
Twitter: www.twitter.com/writeitright7
Blog: www.blogspot.com/primeeventschatterbox
Tumblr: www.upwritesolutions.tumblr
YouTube: www.youtube.com/upwritesolutions

Books by Tonya Franklin:
upwritesolutions.com/InTheSpotlight

Want to know how you could *shape up* your customer service skills?

Need a *quick and easy* training guide to freshen up your employees' customer service skills?

This may be the tool for you!

Included are training modules with real-life scenarios and an action plan to teach and guide you to having great customer service skills.

HAVE **YOU** READ?

go to upwritesolutions.com and click on the button link to order your copy today!

amazon.com
upwritesolutions.com

Interested in getting more out of your book?
Sign up for the e-course...

SHARPEN ME UP

**7 WEEK SELF-STUDY
E-COURSE
ON DEVELOPING GREAT
CUSTOMER SERVICE
SKILLS**

- **E-mailed study lessons**
- **Live chat sessions**
- **Personal journal for jotting notes**

*Enrollment begins
April 1!*

$35

Includes book, journal, & more!

GOOD
CUSTOMER
SERVICE
TIPS FOR
ENTREPRENEURS

PLEASE AND THANK
YOU WITH A SMILE

TONYA FRANKLIN

Get this FREE mini-e book today!
Go to upwritesolutions.com to download your copy.

COMING SOON...

FOX TRAILS:
Handling Conflict in Business, Family & Ministry

COMING SOON...

By The Way Virtual Book Promotions. Are you looking for a platform to advertise your book, magazine, podcast, or TV show?

By The Way will serve as your promotional source for your new media publications!

Stay tuned to the website:
tonyadfranklin.com for more information to come.